★ BE THE **Change!** POLITICAL PARTICIPATION IN YOUR COMMUNITY™ ★

MAKING THE MOST OF COMMUNICATIONS AND SOCIAL MEDIA IN A POLITICAL CAMPAIGN

Angie Timmons

New York

Published in 2020 by The Rosen Publishing Group, Inc.
29 East 21st Street, New York, NY 10010

Copyright © 2020 by The Rosen Publishing Group, Inc.

First Edition

All rights reserved. No part of this book may be reproduced in any form without permission in writing from the publisher, except by a reviewer.

Cataloging-in-Publication Data

Names: Timmons, Angie, author.
Title: Making the most of communications and social media in a political campaign / Angie Timmons.
Description: New York : Rosen Publishing, 2020 | Series: Be the change! : political participation in your community | Includes bibliographical references and index. | Audience: Grades 7–12.
Identifiers: ISBN 9781725340879 (library bound) | ISBN 9781725340862 (pbk.)
Subjects: LCSH: Communication in politics—Technological innovations—United States—Juvenile literature. | Communication in politics—Juvenile literature. | Social media—Political aspects—United States—Juvenile literature. | Political participation—Technological innovations—United States—Juvenile literature. | Internet in political campaigns—United States—Juvenile literature.
Classification: LCC JA85.2.U6 T55 2020 | DDC 324.7'30973—dc23

Manufactured in the United States of America

CONTENTS

INTRODUCTION **4**

CHAPTER ONE
**POLITICAL COMMUNICATIONS
STRATEGIES: THEN AND NOW** **7**

CHAPTER TWO
CAMPAIGN COMMUNICATIONS **20**

CHAPTER THREE
**THE TWENTY-FOUR-HOUR
NEWS CYCLE** **31**

CHAPTER FOUR
CAMPAIGNS AND YOU **42**

GLOSSARY **52**
FOR MORE INFORMATION **54**
FOR FURTHER READING **58**
BIBLIOGRAPHY **59**
INDEX **61**

INTRODUCTION

It was about 83 degrees Fahrenheit (28 degrees Celsius) with 77 percent humidity in the Texas border town of Brownsville on the night of August 18, 2018. US congressman Beto O'Rourke, a Democrat from El Paso, had been on the campaign trail all day in his bid to become the next US senator from Texas. At about 8 p.m., he stopped at the Brownsville Whataburger, a popular Texas fast-food restaurant, to grab dinner. Before eating, however, he borrowed a skateboard from another patron, fired up Facebook Live, and proceeded to skateboard across the Whataburger parking lot. Then he jumped off the skateboard, went into the restaurant, ordered a hamburger, and spent the next thirty minutes livestreaming his conversations with fellow customers.

Within three days, the video had been watched more than 134,000 times, shared more than 1,400 times, retweeted thousands of times, and replayed on newscasts around the world. O'Rourke had been growing in popularity among progressives in Republican-majority Texas due to his grassroots campaigning and passionate political messaging. Those few moments on Facebook Live, however, made him a superstar in Texas and across the country.

While hundreds of political candidates use social media, O'Rourke used it to blast campaign

INTRODUCTION 5

In his 2018 bid for US Senate, Texas congressman Beto O'Rourke took campaign communications to new heights by using in-person and social media tactics.

communications to a whole new level. His campaign didn't have a concrete communications strategy, so he improvised along the way. As he traveled to all 254 Texas counties, he livestreamed multiple times a day and wrote all his own tweets, sharing what he learned about Texans on the campaign trail. He used social media to grow an army of twenty-five thousand campaign volunteers and used Facebook ads (among other digital sources) to raise $70 million—more than any Senate campaign in US history. O'Rourke, who began his campaign in March 2017 with just two aides and a rented sedan, had come a long way. Social media was largely to thank for that.

Political campaign communications has long been big business. Candidates spend thousands, if not millions, on communications experts and advertising. That's because reaching voters is critical to winning an election, and getting voters to support a candidate or even show up to vote is hard work. Moreover, content must be tailored for all kinds of audiences. Candidates must find a way to reach everyone from elderly voters who read print newspapers to young voters who consume information on mobile devices (and typically spend very little time on any one news story).

When Barack Obama first ran for president in 2008, Facebook was only a few years old and Twitter only two years old. Obama realized the voter outreach potential of these new social media tools, giving him an advantage—especially with young voters—over other candidates who were slow to adopt the new technologies. While traditional communications strategies such as newspaper interviews, block walking, and public forums are still used in most political campaigns, the way people expect to interact with candidates changes with every new web-based communications tool. O'Rourke's Snapchats, tweets, Facebook Live updates, and Instagram posts prove that campaign communications isn't just big business anymore—it's a multimedia frenzy.

CHAPTER ONE

POLITICAL COMMUNICATIONS STRATEGIES: THEN AND NOW

In the early days of the United States, publicly campaigning for political office was considered unseemly. In the times before radio, television, telephones, photography, cars, and even railroads, information about political candidates was largely confined to the nation's fledgling print newspapers and political brochures. However, many Americans were illiterate. Outside of populous areas, where information could be shared verbally, the public may have known little to nothing about candidates, even presidential

The flashy political rallies held in today's political campaigns are a far cry from the quiet, "dignified" campaigning conducted by early American politicians.

7

Making the Most of Communications and Social Media in a Political Campaign

BEFORE TWITTER WARS: MUDSLINGING

The quiet, dignified approach to presidential campaigning began to change in 1828. The incumbent candidate, President John Quincy Adams, was wildly unpopular. He went on the offensive in his race against his opponent, former Tennessee senator Andrew Jackson. Adams launched vicious attacks against Jackson via what is called mudslinging, undermining and damaging an opponent's reputation through insults and accusations. Jackson slung right back, accusing Adams of political corruptness. The mudslinging even got personal. Adams called Jackson's marriage immoral because Jackson had courted his wife, Rachel, before her divorce with a previous husband was finalized. The private lives of candidates had previously been kept under wraps, so the attack on Jackson's marriage was shocking. Jackson responded by calling Adams's English wife, Louisa, a foreigner who didn't care about America.

The mudslinging coincided with advances in printing. This new form of media gave rise to political posters and pamphlets, which were widely distributed by the candidates' supporters. While Adams and Jackson maintained the tradition of staying put rather than campaigning on the road, printed materials did their campaigning for them. Newspapers fanned the flames of the

The 1828 presidential race between John Quincy Adams and Andrew Jackson was one of the first to use personal attacks in campaign communications.

contentious campaign by freely printing the candidates' scandalous claims about each other. (Most early nineteenth-century newspapers aligned with a particular political party and did not use unbiased reporting, fact-checking, and corroboration by multiple sources to cover politics. Instead, they wrote in favor of the candidates from the party with which the newspaper was associated.)

Some historians consider the 1828 presidential election the ugliest in American history—a remarkable distinction for a campaign that was primarily limited to printed attack ads and propaganda. Adams and Jackson gave rise to negative political campaigning, which is now a pillar of many campaign communications strategies.

candidates. Many Americans may not have even known what candidates looked like.

In post-Revolutionary America and throughout the nineteenth century, it was customary for presidential candidates to behave as if they were too dignified to campaign. Among early politicians, who had a recent memory of the political idealism that had inspired the American Revolution, campaigning for public office was considered undemocratic; campaigning could give a candidate an unfair advantage over others based on factors like popularity or appearance rather than political skill or values.

In keeping with the no-campaigning custom, early presidential candidates stayed close to home while members of their political party campaigned for them. Presidential nominees didn't make public speeches. They didn't hold rallies. Their private lives remained largely private.

STUMPS AND PORCHES

As the nineteenth century progressed and the United States grew in size, candidates found ways to work around the tradition of keeping up a noble appearance (that is, behaving as if they didn't want to be president in order to maintain an air of dignity) without actually breaking from the custom altogether. In doing so, they began to have direct contact with voters.

STUMPING

In 1836, US senators Hugh Lawson White of Tennessee and Daniel Webster of Massachusetts were two of four Whig Party members vying for the presidential nomination. The newly formed Whig Party didn't hold a national convention and White and Webster needed to find a way to appeal to their fellow party members and voters. In what are sometimes considered the first incidents of presidential candidate stumping, White and Webster used their Senate debates, which were printed in national newspapers, to share their political views. (The term "stumping" refers to delivering public addresses. It derives from the practice of giving speeches from atop a tree stump, which political party members like Andrew Jackson did on behalf of their party's presidential nominee.)

Although they failed to win the presidency, White and Webster introduced a major break from the tradition of refraining from public rhetoric in pursuit of political office. Candidates continued to stump, although the practice was still frowned upon in the nineteenth century. In a 1988 *New York Times* letter to the editor, historian Gil Troy noted that in the nineteenth century, stumping was "thought undignified—and unwise. Presidential candidates, especially after

In the early twentieth century, President Theodore Roosevelt took advantage of trains by traveling great distances to deliver campaign speeches and meet voters.

nomination, were supposed to stand, not run, for election." Some candidates would find pretexts for their public appearances in order to avoid the stigma of stumping. One candidate, spotted by members of the public while traveling, expressed surprise and condemned stumping, but then proceeded to deliver a public address on the spot.

The growing availability of railroad travel in the late nineteenth century gave stumping more speed. President Theodore Roosevelt, who served as president from 1901 to 1909, famously traversed the country by rail, addressing crowds from a train car. Candidates could make multiple public appearances in one day using trains.

FRONT PORCH POLITICS

Beginning in the 1880s, presidential campaigns began to show signs of sophisticated communications strategies, often informed by powerful people who backed a presidential candidate. This included a new form of communicating with the public called front porch campaigning, in which members of the public and reporters were invited to visit candidates at their homes. Perhaps the most famous example of front porch campaigning is the 1896 presidential campaign of Republican William McKinley. Thousands of curious Americans, voters, and news reporters flocked to McKinley's Ohio home to see him and have the opportunity to talk to him. This surge of interest was largely due to the work of a wealthy McKinley supporter, Mark Hanna, who amassed donations from other supporters to deliver the first full-fledged political media campaign. Hanna hired 1,400 people to photograph McKinley and ensure those photos were widely circulated. He even struck a deal with rail companies to offer discount fares to anyone who wanted to visit McKinley in Ohio. It worked—McKinley won the presidency.

Front porch campaigning eliminated the uncertainty of travel (rail travel had grown, but it was slow and not available everywhere) and was considered more dignified than stumping. A candidate's front porch was also a more controlled environment; unlike on a stumping tour, candidates didn't have to depend on relative strangers to introduce them to delegations. For the most part, candidates didn't give speeches in front porch campaigning, but rather held conversations with their visitors.

McKinley's front porch campaigning wasn't unique only in the way he interacted with voters, but also in how he managed to encourage thousands of people to travel long distances to see him. Thanks to his wealthy friend Hanna, McKinley's campaign is one of the first obvious examples of a big-money interest influencing a campaign strategy and a campaign outcome—influences that are now regular parts of high-profile political campaigns.

FROM IDEALISM TO THE INEVITABLE

Stumping, front porch chats, and railcar speeches were not exactly in keeping with the campaigns envisioned by the idealistic Founding Fathers. They were, however, an inevitable result of the need for politicians to get to know a nation that had grown beyond the Founding Fathers' wildest dreams.

Unlike the quiet, early days of campaigning, public appearances allowed voters to not only see the candidate, but also to learn more about their political stances and ideas—which was especially useful in reaching rural areas and voters who could not read. Hitting the campaign trail also gave candidates better insight into the issues various communities faced, allowing them to make plans for policy.

MODERN MODES

The 1920s brought campaigning into the early home electronics age. The advent of radio technologies allowed candidates to share their messages with large segments of the population. By the 1950s, presidential candidates began to appear on television, giving voters the opportunity not only to see and listen to candidates, but also to learn more about their stances and personalities. In 1960, Democrat John F. Kennedy and Republican Richard Nixon faced off in the first-ever televised presidential debate. The debate was met with conflicting perceptions: those who listened to it on the radio believed Nixon had prevailed, while those who watched it on television thought Kennedy had taken the debate. This disparity in opinion was the first true

indication of how the public perceived a candidate's physical appearance; while Nixon sweated profusely and appeared pale, Kennedy looked the picture of health. Kennedy was victorious in the presidential race against Nixon. Now, televised debates are an expected part of presidential campaigns and some high-profile congressional campaigns. At the state and local level,

Republican Richard Nixon faced off against Democrat John F. Kennedy in the first-ever televised presidential debate. Nixon's negative appearance on television lost him some public support.

candidates will often debate and may even do so on local television channels or online.

HITTING THE ROAD

Modern political candidates face communications expectations on a scale their predecessors could not have even imagined. High-profile political campaigns include frequent public appearances to meet voters, raise funds, attend rallies and events, give speeches, debate opponents, meet with civic and business leaders, and promote their brand through things like book tours and media campaigns. Presidential candidates may campaign in multiple cities or even states in a single day. The busy campaign schedules of presidential candidates may soon be a part of the communications strategies for candidates running for other offices.

THE MEDIA MACHINE

When not in legislative session, federal and state elected officials spend most of their time campaigning to win the next election. This means communicating with the public through any means available,

Political Communications Strategies: Then and Now

including online. Big-league-style campaigning is no longer restricted to high-profile campaigns. The prevalence of social media and its ability to reach many people quickly has brought even small-time candidates online. Candidates know that the internet provides an efficient way to reach voters; after all, the first thing most people do when they want to learn more about someone or something is conduct an internet search.

Today's political candidates can expect to be followed by huge groups of news reporters and photographers who document their every move to feed the twenty-four-hour media machine.

A NEW WAY OF DOING THINGS?

Leading up to the November 6, 2018, midterm elections, Beto O'Rourke crisscrossed the second-largest state, Texas, to visit voters in every county. He visited tiny rural towns and massive urban centers alike. Many of the rural counties he visited had not been visited by a major political candidate since Lyndon B. Johnson, a Texan who served as US president from 1963 to 1969.

O'Rourke may have lost to incumbent Republican senator Ted Cruz, but he did so by a slim margin (three points), coming closer to the Senate than any Texas Democrat had in decades. For this reason and for several others, many experts view O'Rourke's campaign as a success. Not only did O'Rourke inspire members of Texas's minority political party to rally in huge numbers, his hands-on campaigning encouraged high voter turnout overall—especially among young voters, a typically difficult voter group to motivate.

In a November 9, 2018, *Guardian* article, Bethany Albertson, a professor at the University of Texas, explained what O'Rourke accomplished with his extensive and innovative campaigning: "If you look at the top line and see O'Rourke losing, you're missing the point. No Democrat has come close in Texas in decades, voter turnout was way up, and young people who have never voted before were drawn for the first time into the democratic process."

Another way to look at the support O'Rourke inspired is the fact that the millions of dollars he raised were mostly through small donations from individual supporters. This is markedly different from many high-profile candidates and politicians, who take large sums of money from corporations or special interest groups.

Between his donor record, his campaign style, and his incredibly communicative style—which made voters feel like they were truly part of his campaign—O'Rourke created a completely new campaign style and may very well have ushered in a new era of political campaigning.

CHAPTER TWO

CAMPAIGN COMMUNICATIONS

Regardless of the office for which they are running or how they reach out to voters, candidates absolutely must communicate with the public. Why? Because informing voters about a candidate's stances on relevant issues is hands down the most important part of a campaign. However, getting voters to back a candidate isn't done through the candidate's stances alone. Those stances must be communicated to the public in the most effective way possible. Creating the right communications strategy can require outside help.

COMPREHENSIVE COMMUNICATIONS

Candidates and their campaign teams have to figure out the best ways to reach a lot of different types of voters—and make sure the candidates look and sound good, considering that the prevalence of politics on screens has increased substantially since the 1960 Kennedy-Nixon debate. Online video services like

Campaign Communications | **21**

YouTube and livestreaming on social media have given politicians and candidates even more avenues to speak directly to the public or go live from the campaign trail. Successful campaign websites and social media profiles require well-written content detailing key issues, ideas for policy, and biographical information, as well as photos and videos of the candidates.

Through mediums like television and the internet, candidates' personal lives have taken more of a central role than in generations past. Many candidates post photos of their families and share details about their personal and professional backgrounds. A strong

Candidates often use their personal lives to relate to everyday voters. Sometimes they bring their families on the campaign trail or feature them online to show they understand family values.

professional or political background, wholesome family life, or compelling personal story can help candidates gain voter support. Depending on the candidate, one or more of these characteristics will be central to defining the candidate's public persona.

Because of technology, modern candidates' lives are on full display, for better or for worse. Some candidates fail because they made a mistake that went viral or because negative information about them was leaked. Other candidates succeed because they have no secrets or, more likely, because they enlisted the help of experts to control the narrative. All of these needs, from effectively reaching voters to maintaining a positive public profile, fall under campaign communications.

BRINGING IN THE EXPERTS

Political candidates learned a lot from Nixon's appearance and performance during that first televised debate, which has been repeatedly documented as a turning point in campaign communications. Today, it would be strange to see a presidential candidate making the same mistakes. Savvy candidates know how important it is to look good while also sounding competent enough for the job, and they know they probably can't do it all on their own.

Campaign Communications 23

Savvy candidates hire teams of full-time consultants who mold nearly every aspect of their campaign life, from what clothes they wear to how they talk.

To put their best face forward, many candidates hire communications specialists or consultants to handle their campaign communications strategy and deployment. High-profile candidates, like those running for president, Congress, governor,

WHAT DOES A CAMPAIGN COMMUNICATIONS SPECIALIST DO?

Most political campaigns will designate someone to be director of communications. That person will oversee most or all aspects of the campaign's communications strategy. Communications directors cultivate relationships with the media and act as spokespeople for the campaign. They will create a content strategy based on campaign events and days of national or local interest and help the candidate respond to current events and the actions of opposing candidates. Communications directors often have a background in writing, which is useful in creating campaign literature like mailers, speeches, scripts, and website content, or come from a communications-heavy profession, like marketing or advertising. They'll work with other members of the campaign team to create a content strategy and to develop content that effectively reflects the candidate and his or her vision for public service.

Communications specialists are expected to be proficient in using social media. This skill includes analyzing data to figure out key pieces of information, such as what time of day a candidate's Twitter followers are online in large numbers. This helps communications specialists plan social media posts.

Political communications and marketing consultants get even more involved in high-profile campaigns in which a candidate's physical appearance and overall image are of great significance. These experts sometimes reinvent or adjust a candidate's image to better appeal to voters. For instance, they may suggest a candidate wear glasses to look more intelligent. They'll fine-tune a candidate's public persona, advising the candidate on everything from wardrobe to public speaking. Depending on the candidate and the election, these consultants may have a lot of control over a candidate's image—and the overall campaign.

or state legislature, commonly hire a marketing or communications firm that can provide the candidate with a team of people who have a wide range of expertise. These firms can offer or arrange services like website and social media management, arranging news interviews and media appearances, writing (press releases, website content, and social media content), photography, videography, and analytics that let the campaign team know how effective its communications are. Smaller political campaigns may have just one person to oversee communications and advise the candidate, while other duties, such as photography or videography, are handled by other members of the campaign team or volunteers.

ON THE LOCAL LEVEL

Candidates for local offices, like mayor, city council, or school board, usually do not have as extensive communications needs as those running for Congress or state offices, though there are exceptions. For example, local candidates running in big cities, where the race for mayor or city council may be very high profile, get a lot of attention from the media and the public. Candidates in some smaller cities may find themselves needing the help of a communications specialist or team, especially if they're in a local race that is contentious or if they're running for an elected position in which they would have a lot of power over something the public cares about, like tax rates. Communications expertise may be helpful for local candidates running in an area that has an active

TRADITIONAL ROUTES

Not all campaign communications happen online. Candidates still rely on traditional communications methods to reach voters and encourage positive word of mouth. These include direct mail, advertising, media interviews, and physical media such as yard signs and door hangers. These methods are vital to increase a candidate's name recognition.

Volunteers for campaigns of all sizes actually play a vital communications role by doing field work like block walking (where volunteers and sometimes the candidates themselves knock on the doors of private homes to meet the electorate) and phone banking (wherein the campaign calls members of the public directly). This field work gives voters and potential voters the chance to personally interact with campaigns and learn more about the candidates. It also gives candidates an important opportunity to learn more about the people they hope to

Campaign teams visit residents in the districts where candidates hope to get elected. This face-to-face interaction is an invaluable source of information and a good way to build trust.

represent as an elected official. Before block walking or phone banking, a candidate may not have known about the many things the public cares about. For instance, a candidate may not have known that a neighborhood in the district was experiencing higher than usual crime rates or that parents were concerned about what their children were learning in school. Candidates can take what they learn from these interactions and turn it into messaging that reflects what the public cares about.

Traditional campaign communication methods like advertising and printed materials can be expensive. Field work can be time consuming and tiring. However, putting in the time and money is worth it because these methods reach people who may not have reliable internet access, who may have limited knowledge of elections and candidates, or who may simply need a reminder that an election's coming up. Moreover, the value of personally interacting with voters and learning what they need and what they care about is priceless.

electorate (such as areas with many senior citizens, who tend to be politically active), comprised of voters who pay attention to news and politics and demand to know how candidates plan to use their time in office.

KEEPING UP WITH THE TIMES

As communications methods evolve, so must the candidates who depend on communications to gain public support. This means adapting to new technologies such as social media. Cris Haest, founder of the Dallas-based marketing firm Bright Social Agency, specializes in social media and has managed political campaigns' communications strategies. She says social media is critical in connecting candidates with voters—both the populace at large and specific

Thanks to livestreaming and social media, candidates can share campaign events with unlimited numbers of people and speak directly to the public in real time.

interest groups (such as groups aligned with a candidate's political party). Social media's potential is remarkable because it can help a candidate "reach around the world in minutes," according to Haest in an interview with the author. But social media is useful for more than just reaching out to the public and asking them to vote for a candidate. It can also be used to broadcast and organize volunteer activities and campaign events, helping people who want to get involved find a way to do so.

Social media has also given candidates direct access to voters—access that used to be limited to avenues like public appearances and news interviews. Social media allows campaigns to "easily share a candidate's stance on topics, even as those topics are breaking headlines, without the need to wait for a reporter to connect with your staff for an interview or the cameras to be rolling. It helps increase the ability to communicate with all possible voters and allow candidates the ability to see in real time how their constituents feel and are affected by all topics," Haest said.

While Haest believes traditional news (newspapers and television news) will likely always have a place in politics, there's no question that social media has forever changed political campaigning communications. Because it's usually free or inexpensive, social media is a cost-effective way for candidates to communicate, allowing even minor candidates with small budgets the opportunity to reach out to voters. Because so many people use social media, it's an invaluable way for candidates to reach a lot of people at once and build a following of people who will hopefully vote for them on Election Day. And because social media provides direct communication between candidates and the public, candidates no longer have to rely solely on traditional methods to inform voters about their priorities and ideas.

WHY CAMPAIGN COMMUNICATIONS MATTER

A political candidate's communication with the public can take a lot of different forms, but the goal of all campaign communications is to successfully persuade voters to support a candidate based on factors such as personality and campaign platform (how a candidate intends to address issues people care about). Campaign communications, whether conducted in person, through news interviews, or on social media, give people insight into candidates and their views and ideas. Additionally, how candidates communicate during a campaign can be a great indication of how they plan to serve if elected to office. They can prove (or disprove) that they are attentive, responsive, and committed to serving the public by demonstrating those traits on the campaign trail. Accessible candidates will likely be accessible elected officials. This is important to note because elected officials work for you.

CHAPTER THREE

THE TWENTY-FOUR-HOUR NEWS CYCLE

Serious political candidates, especially those running for high-profile offices, must be in nearly constant communication with the public. This means around-the-clock engagement with the public and prompt responses to current events and headlines. Some reasons for this include the evolution of twenty-four-hour news channels and the introduction of social media. Voters can be online at any time of the day or night, looking for candidates' latest communications about everything from political stances to reactions to breaking news. They can watch cable news stations that operate around the clock—a phenomenon that candidates from previous generations could not have even imagined. With twenty-four hours to fill, these cable news stations feature everything from actual news reporting to opinion-heavy programs hosted by commentators who have political agendas. Between the internet and cable news, the public can be looking for information about politics day and night.

The twenty-four-hour news cycle has given rise to constant reporting and commentary about politics, particularly on cable news stations.

CONSTANT CONTACT

Constant communication between candidates and the public can be a positive thing. It allows people to access candidate information and communications at their convenience and shows voters whether candidates are paying attention to and responding to issues and current events in a timely fashion. Campaign websites that detail candidate qualifications and stances give voters the opportunity to research candidates at their convenience. Blogs and YouTube videos give the public insight into candidates' platforms

The Twenty-Four-Hour News Cycle

We're a long way from railcar stumping now. Modern candidates and voters can access each other around the clock simply by turning on the television or pulling out their phones.

without having to attend rallies, events, or fundraisers or wait for the news media to profile specific candidates. Social media gives candidates the opportunity to craft their messaging in a succinct way and share it on campaign Facebook, Twitter, Instagram, Snapchat, and video accounts. Going live on Facebook or Instagram gives candidates the chance to give the public real-time access to them and their campaigns. It's never been easier for the public to find out about elections, issues, elected officials, and candidates, and it's never been easier for candidates to ask for the public's support by sharing their vision for the future over all these different mediums.

OPINION VS. NEWS

There are downsides to the twenty-four-hour news cycle. The expectation of constant communication can lead to programming that features opinion masquerading as news. Understandably, many people believe what they hear on the news because they trust the news to provide them with accurate, thorough information. However, to fill time slots in the around-the-clock news cycle and appeal to specific segments of the population, twenty-four-hour cable news channels often feature programs that deal with current events but are hosted by commentators who editorialize (expressing opinions rather than simply reporting the news). Many cable news organizations have openly admitted their political bias; for instance, Fox News doesn't hide its conservatism (more friendly toward the Republican Party) and MSNBC is noticeably liberal (associated more with the Democratic Party). These biases are so apparent that you can often guess the way people vote based on where they get their news.

Candidates who share news stories from one-sided sources probably do so only to support their own views rather than to take a hard look at what the public at large thinks. That's an unfortunate characteristic that they may bring into public office if they're not held accountable by the public.

CRAFTING THE MESSAGE

The concept of candidates sharing their political opinions and ideas with the public sounds straightforward. After all, by the time most candidates announce they're running for office, they've likely spent time identifying key issues and developing campaign platforms based on those issues. They've thought about what they want to do about those issues if they're elected. Candidates may adjust their priorities based on what they learn and experience on the campaign trail, but their goals for campaign communications remain the same: highlighting their positive attributes and ideas while ignoring or minimizing the things they don't want voters to focus on. This is called political messaging—crafting the story that candidates want to tell the voters.

(CONTINUED ON THE NEXT PAGE)

Donald Trump used crafty campaign messaging to undermine his opponents and rally supporters—even though he lacked specific policy ideas for his presidency.

> **(CONTINUED FROM THE PREVIOUS PAGE)**
>
> It seems logical that candidates would focus on the good stuff and highlight their positive attributes. Unfortunately, candidates (and the public) can get swept up in the rosy-colored messaging a candidate repeats without realizing some things are being left out. In the 2016 presidential race, Republican candidate Donald Trump repeatedly criticized and promised to repeal the Affordable Care Act (ACA), a health care bill passed under Democratic president Barack Obama. The bill was unpopular with some Americans. Trump targeted those people, rallying them around criticism of the legislation. However, he neglected to propose a solid alternative policy to the ACA. Trump mastered political messaging by highlighting what his supporters thought was something positive (promises to repeal the ACA) while successfully ignoring and drawing attention away from what his promises lacked (an alternative to the ACA). Trump was elected, but his failure to develop an alternative to the ACA plagued his presidency. He'd successfully told voters the story he wanted them to hear, but it wasn't the whole story.

WATCH OUT FOR FAKE NEWS

A term that's regularly thrown around by modern-day politicians and political commentators, "fake news" refers to propaganda or what used to be called yellow journalism—illegitimate and poorly researched news with sensational headlines to draw in readers. In the late nineteenth and early twentieth centuries, yellow journalism was common between warring newspapers that competed for readership and ad sales. Some newspapers or reporters would even pay sources for information. However, due to the blatant misinformation and panic caused by yellow journalism, it eventually fell out of practice, giving way to enhanced journalistic standards intended to level the playing field and gain the public's trust through accurate information.

In recent decades, the internet and social media have led to the reintroduction of fake news. Most websites rely on advertising revenue to stay in business, and advertisers pay to be featured on websites that get a lot of traffic. To increase traffic and keep the advertisement money coming in, organizations with a political agenda and even some mainstream news sites have adopted some old yellow journalism tactics, repurposed for the digital age.

Yellow journalism has found a new home online, where everything from mainstream news sites to agenda-specific blogs sensationalize news headlines to grab readers and ad revenue.

These include attention-grabbing headlines intended to attract readers to click through to a story (called clickbait) and articles that read like news stories but are in fact opinion pieces.

THE SOCIAL MEDIA MAELSTROM

On social media, algorithms (automated reasoning calculations based on a particular formula) allow bots (a program or network that operates without human oversight) to target users with information based on those users' trends. For instance, someone who often searches for news about Republican candidates will be presented with "news" about Republicans by bots that share on a mass scale what their algorithms tell them will be of interest to that particular social media user—without regard for the quality or source of the information being shared. Therefore, fake news can be shared on an incredible scale. This is dangerous, considering that 62 percent of adult Americans get their news from social media (according to a 2016 study by the Pew Research Center), and considering that the public (and even some candidates) use social media as their primary way of discovering and discussing politics.

Social media expert Cris Haest said that while social media has expanded the way politicians and candidates connect with the community, it has also "become a weapon to help take down people on the opposing side via smear campaigns turned trending topics, to help enlarge and encompass echo chambers that both help with progress and help with enraging those that choose an anger- or fear-based response."

While fake news is technically propaganda or yellow journalism reinvented for the digital era, the term itself has been used incorrectly to undermine legitimate news sources. For example, during his presidency, President Donald Trump attempted to cast doubt on legitimate news organizations that reported anything negative about him by calling them "fake news" sources. He even went so far as to refuse interviews with or banish reporters from major mainstream news organizations that he deemed "fake news" just because they'd reported something he perceived as critical of him.

However, social media isn't all bad when it comes to politics. Haest says that social media can be used as a "way to help create some sense of accountability" for politicians. For example, devices like smartphones can be used to photograph, film, and record candidates and share their words and actions with the world over social media. This permanent record makes it harder for politicians to deny their words and actions.

WHAT'S REAL?

The 2016 presidential election saw an unprecedented level of traditional news sources being bypassed altogether as candidates made their campaign websites and social media accounts primary sources of news about the election and their candidacies. This means they controlled the messaging, rather than allowing traditional news sources that rely on journalistic standards to inform the public and provide more perspective.

Traditional news sources are more trustworthy than most internet-based "news" sources because their reporters use ethical practices to report the news in an unbiased, fact-based manner.

Knowing what's real, fake, opinion, fact, and actual journalism versus controlled messaging is challenging, but there are ways to see through all the information out there. If a candidate shares a news story, assess the

The Twenty-Four-Hour News Cycle

news source: read multiple stories to see if that particular news organization takes care to get interviews with various sources to show all sides of the issue and provides facts to support the information it shares, or if it seems to tell only one side of the story. If a news source is telling only one side of the story, that's a sign that it's reporting more opinion than news.

With so much information available about any one issue, candidates have plenty of reputable news sources they can use to share information. In doing so, they can make the most of today's enhanced communications methods to share accurate information and inspire a real conversation about important issues with voters. If a candidate posts about an issue based on a solid, fact-checked, corroborated news story from a source with a good reputation, then that candidate can probably be trusted to deal with facts and evidence when developing policy ideas that impact you, your future, and the people and issues you care about.

CHAPTER FOUR

CAMPAIGNS AND YOU

Leading up to the 2016 presidential election, Republican candidate Donald Trump (a businessman and reality television star with no political experience) seemed an unlikely candidate to triumph over his opponent, Democratic candidate Hillary Clinton. As former secretary of state and US senator, she brought substantial diplomatic and governmental experience to the table.

Trump relied on social media to undermine his opponent. Using strong language and bold claims (often unsubstantiated) on Twitter, he successfully rallied many voters to share his point of view that Clinton was an untrustworthy candidate who was ill suited for the presidency by repeatedly bringing up her alleged failures and by attacking the Democratic Party for controversial Obama-era legislation such as the Affordable Care Act (ACA). Though Clinton won the popular vote, Trump won the electoral college vote and thus the presidency. Social media is at least partially

Donald Trump, who was often erratic and inflammatory during his presidential race against Hillary Clinton in 2016, used mass media to persuade voters that Clinton was a bad choice.

responsible for turning this unlikely candidate into the president of the United States.

CAMPAIGNS IN THE DIGITAL ERA

The 2016 presidential race shows just how much campaign communications have changed since the days of Andrew Jackson's "stumping," Theodore Roosevelt's speeches from train cars, and the grainy, black-and-white televised debate between Kennedy and Nixon. The public has gone from expecting occasional access to candidates to expecting almost constant access. Candidates share content and images on almost everything: in the course of a single day, a candidate may post a picture of his or her lunch on Instagram, publish a heartfelt blog post about why he or she is running for office on the campaign

The lives of political candidates may be documented almost constantly on social media and reproduced in campaign materials like websites or fliers.

website, and post several reactions to current events on Facebook and Twitter.

All of this is calculated. The lunch post shows the candidate supports a local business. The blog post highlights the candidate's positive qualities or elicits an emotional response from readers, while using keywords (such as "health care" or "gun reform") increases the likelihood the post will show up in internet searches and reach a wide audience. Responding to news headlines on Facebook and Twitter allows candidates to use current events as a launchpad to discuss their own political ideas, while utilizing hashtags to ride the coattails of trending topics and other social media accounts that are getting a lot of traffic.

Without a robust communications presence, voters may feel disconnected from candidates and elections. That disconnect can turn into poor voter turnout or a candidate's unpopularity among the electorate. To truly connect with the public, candidates need strong written and visual presences across all forms of campaign communications. This can be a round-the-clock duty for many candidates and their campaign teams. To make the most of communications and social media, candidates and their teams must plan content ahead of time and be available to respond to breaking news.

CAMPAIGNS, COMMUNICATIONS, AND YOU

Just because you might not be able to vote yet doesn't mean there's no place for you in politics and communications. In fact, you probably know more

A FUTURE JOB IN POLITICAL COMMUNICATIONS?

To adequately communicate with the public, candidates need a lot of written and visual content that will be on everything from yard signs to YouTube. Therefore, people with backgrounds in journalism, marketing, photography, graphic design, and videography are valuable to campaigns because they can skillfully communicate a candidate's message. However, campaign communications aren't limited to people who can write, take photos, or draw. The field of political communications is diverse, and as technology evolves, so does the need for a wide range of experts. The 2016 presidential election showed how powerful social media is, so there's a growing demand for social media experts who can make a candidate's social media presence effective.

While candidates increasingly use social media to share their message and attract supporters, they still have websites that require management. A candidate in a local or state race might just need a webmaster to add content to a campaign website that was built using a template. A higher-profile candidate may look for people who can code a website's design from scratch as well as manage it. People who are experts in protecting against cybercrime are also in increasing demand. An investigation conducted by the Federal Bureau of Investigation in March 2019 found that the 2016 presidential election was influenced by interference from the Russian government, largely through misinformation shared over social media and computer hacking. People who can protect the democratic process are needed in campaigns and politics.

Most colleges offer courses that many campaign communications specialists need, such as journalism, web design, and photography, but many are also increasingly offering social media specializations and even cybercrime-related courses. With campaigns needing such a diverse set of skills, perhaps your career interest will lead you to the ever-changing and always-interesting world of political campaigns.

about social media and technology than many of the adults who currently hold public office. Because politicians make decisions that impact you now, and because they make decisions that will impact your future, you have every right to get involved in politics and communicate with elected officials and candidates. This can increase the chances that something you care about will become a key issue that candidates address through legislation or on the campaign trail.

One great example of this is the March for Our Lives movement, started by high school students at Marjory Stoneman Douglas High School in Parkland,

Teenage survivors of a 2018 mass shooting at a high school in Parkland, Florida, used their social media skills to jump-start a massive and popular movement aimed at gun reform.

Florida. After surviving a mass shooting at their school in February 2018, this group of high schoolers started a nationwide campaign for tighter gun control legislation. Five weeks after the shooting, they organized a march in Washington, DC, which attracted an estimated two hundred thousand people, according to CBS News. Satellite marches around the world showed widespread support for the survivors and the political campaign they started.

As support for the teen-led campaign grew, so did the number of candidates willing to address the issue of gun control. In the 2018 midterm elections, many candidates shared information from March for Our Lives, showing that the work of those young people truly helped to set a political agenda. This is a great example of young people, many of whom were not old enough to vote, making their voices heard in the political arena and demanding that elected officials and candidates pay attention.

START LOCALLY

The March for Our Lives founders gained national attention in their response to a national problem (gun violence). However, making your voice heard can be done a lot closer to home, by getting to know your local governmental bodies, like city councils and school boards. The elected officials who serve on your local government need to know the people they serve. You and your peers are among those people.

Don't stop at the people who have already been elected in your area, your state, or to represent

Campaigns and You

you in Congress; also look into candidates running in upcoming elections. It's always a good time to begin learning more about your school board, city council, county commissioner, state legislature, congressional, and presidential candidates. Now you have the tools to take a hard look at their campaign communications and determine whether they use distortion techniques and fake news to drum up support. If they do, you can hold them accountable by asking them to discuss actual issues and their specific ideas to address them, rather than relying on dishonest tactics to win support.

GET INVOLVED NOW

You can get involved in campaign communications for student government elections or by volunteering for local, state, and even federal campaigns in your area. Chances are, you have an academic or personal skill—like writing, photography, web design, or interpersonal skills—that can be of use to someone running for political office. Gareth Morgans, a political campaign adviser who's worked on fifteen campaigns, shared this advice:

> Political campaigns are always looking for student organizers, volunteers, and Get Out the Vote (GOTV) squads. Find a candidate that you feel best shares your principles and contact their campaign. Ask to speak to a field organizer and explain why you're supporting the candidate and what skills you have that you feel would benefit the campaign.

Getting involved in political campaign communications now can help you a great deal down the line, whether you decide to make your career in politics or not. The connections you make while working on a political campaign can serve you well in the future; you can ask your contacts for letters of reference for jobs or college applications and rely on that network for help finding jobs related to your skills or interests. The experience you gain on a campaign can help you build your portfolio of work, which you can use in college applications, job applications, and as the beginning of your physical or digital portfolio (especially important for writers, photographers, videographers, graphic designers, and web designers). You'll gain impressive

Young people have a big role to play in political campaigns. They can put their energy and skills to good use while simultaneously building a network of valuable resources.

real-world experience and meet people who share your interests and values.

IT'S IN YOUR HANDS NOW

In the book *See How They Run: Campaign Dreams, Election Schemes, and the Race to the White House*, authors Susan E. Goodman and Elwood H. Smith raise some good questions about how much exposure the modern public has to candidates: "Is this for better or worse? Are we getting to know our candidates as people or are they playing a part? Do we need to know our candidates as people? That's for us to decide. Democracy is a messy business and it's our job to sort it out."

   Soon, you'll have a say in who's elected to public office. As you reach voting age, use the tools you've learned to decipher candidate communications and decide whom you support. Even if you can't yet vote, you can still volunteer for campaigns, share candidate communications on social media, and do field work to encourage voters to support your chosen candidates. Most importantly, you can begin making informed decisions about politics and holding candidates and elected officials accountable by demanding that they communicate effectively and honestly. Now that you know what to look for in a campaign's political messaging, you can help others read between the lines and decide whom they want making decisions for them. Take control of your future by getting involved in politics even before you can vote. Democracy may be messy, but your future depends on its integrity and its success.

GLOSSARY

analytics The analysis of data or statistics, often used to make decisions about strategy.
bias Prejudice in favor of or against one thing, person, or group.
campaign To work toward the goal of getting elected to a public office.
candidate A person who runs for public office.
communications Sharing or exchanging information and news.
corroboration When information is verified, confirmed, and substantiated by facts and multiple sources.
election A process in which a group of people vote.
electoral college A body of electors (representatives from each state) convened every four years to elect the president and vice president of the United States.
electorate The people who are entitled to vote in an election.
grassroots A type of organizational structure, such as a campaign, that mobilizes individuals rather than established organizations to participate in helping to achieve a specific outcome (like getting a candidate elected).
incumbent The candidate who currently holds an elected office and is seeking reelection.
legislation Considering and making laws as part of a governing body.
legislature The legislative body of a country or state.
media The collective means of mass communications, including broadcasting, publishing, and the internet.

Glossary

midterm election An election in which voters can elect representatives and other officeholders (such as state representatives or members of a local council) in the middle of the executive officer's term.

nominee A candidate who is officially chosen to run for office (often by a political party).

platform The stated policy or policies of a political party, group, or candidate.

political party A group of people who work together because they share similar ideas.

politician A person who runs for or holds a political office.

popular vote The votes cast by the actual electorate in a presidential election (as opposed to the electoral college).

propaganda Biased or misleading information used to promote or publicize a particular political point of view.

public office A position within the government that involves being responsible to the public.

reputable Having a good, respected reputation.

voter A person who has the right to cast a vote in an election.

FOR MORE INFORMATION

Arena
Website: http://www.arena.run
Email: hello@thearena.run
Facebook, Twitter, and Instagram: @arenasummit
Arena trains and supports the next generation of campaign staff and candidates. Arena helps first-time candidates enter the political arena through coaching and a comprehensive campaign toolbox for new candidates and campaign staff, as well as offering summits to build relationships.

Canadian Alliance of Student Associations (CASA)
130 Slater Street, Suite 410
Ottawa, ON, K1P 6E2
Canada
Website: http://www.casa-acae.com
Facebook, Instagram, and Twitter: @CASAACAE
CASA is a nonpartisan nonprofit student organization composed of multiple student associations from across Canada. The organization advocates for students, and Canada's leaders consult with CASA on decisions affecting the education system.

Inspire Democracy
30 Victoria Street
Gatineau, QC K1A 0M6
Canada
(800) 463-6868
Website: http://www.inspirerlademocratie
    -inspiredemocracy.ca
Facebook: @ElectionsCanE

For More Information 55

Twitter: @ElectionsCan_E

Inspire Democracy, an initiative of Elections Canada, aims to encourage youth civic engagement. The organization provides information on everything from voter turnout and voter registration data to civic participation and how political parties engage with youth.

Millennial Action Project (MAP)
1875 Connecticut Avenue NW, 10th Floor
Washington, DC 20009
(202) 480-2051
Website: http://www.millennialaction.org
Facebook: @MillennialActionProject
Twitter: @MActionProject

MAP is the largest nonpartisan organization of millennial policymakers in the United States. The organization works to overcome partisanship through future-focused challenges and democracy reforms.

National Democratic Institute (NDI)
455 Massachusetts Avenue NW, 8th Floor
Washington, DC 20001
(202) 728-5500
Website: http://www.ndi.org
Facebook: @National.Democratic.Institute
Instagram: @ndidemocracy
Twitter: @NDI

NDI is a nonprofit nonpartisan organization that supports democratic institutions and practices all over the world. NDI promotes openness and accountability in government by building political and civic organizations, safeguarding elections, and promoting citizen participation.

New Politics
Website: http://www.newpolitics.org
Facebook: @joinnewpolitics
Instagram: @newpolitics
Twitter: @new_poli
New Politics recruits and develops new leaders dedicated to community and country. The organization helps young candidates by providing campaign infrastructure, mentorship, and support.

Reboot Democracy
Website: http://www.rebootdem.com
Facebook, Instagram, and Twitter: @RebootDem
This nonprofit creates a comprehensive ecosystem of support for early-stage innovators who are building technology to strengthen democracy. The organization helps other innovative groups and individuals, especially women and minorities, to connect and collaborate.

Rock the Vote
1440 G Street NW
Washington, DC 20005
(202) 719-9910
Website: https://www.rockthevote.org
Facebook, Instagram, and Twitter: @rockthevote
Rock the Vote is a nonpartisan and progressive nonprofit organization that uses music, pop culture, and art to motivate young people to get involved in

politics, build their political power, and make voting work for everyone.

Youth Service America (YSA)
1050 Connecticut Avenue NW, #65525
Washington, DC 20035-5525
(202) 296-2992
Websites: http://ysa.org or http://leadasap.ysa.org
Email: outreach@ysa.org
Facebook: @youthserviceamerica
Twitter: @youthservice
YSA supports a global culture of engaged children and youth committed to a lifetime of meaningful service, learning, and leadership. The YSA websites feature the stories of young people who make a difference in their communities and give newcomers opportunities to make a difference on their own.

FOR FURTHER READING

Donovan, Sandra. *Media: From News Coverage to Political Advertising*. Minneapolis, MN: Lerner Publications, 2016.

Jacobs, Natalie, and Thomas A. Jacobs. *Every Vote Matters: The Power of Your Voice, from Student Elections to the Supreme Court*. Minneapolis, MN: Free Spirit Publishing, 2016.

Keppeler, Jill. *The Media's Role in Democracy*. New York, NY: Rosen Publishing, 2019.

Lane, Paul. *Viral News on Social Media*. New York, NY: Rosen Publishing, 2019.

Mapua, Jeff. *A Career as a Social Media Manager*. New York, NY: Rosen Publishing, 2018.

Martin, Bobi. *What Are Elections?* New York, NY: Rosen Publishing, 2016.

New York Times editorial staff. *Fake News*. New York, NY: Rosen Publishing, 2019.

New York Times editorial staff. *Identity Politics*. New York, NY: Rosen Publishing, 2019.

Scardino, Franco. *The Complete Idiot's Guide to US Government and Politics*. Indianapolis, IN: DK Publishing, 2016.

Weiss, Nancy E. *Asking Questions About Political Campaigns*. Ann Arbor, MI: Cherry Lake Publishing, 2016.

BIBLIOGRAPHY

Brevard, Katherine McLean, and Davis Worth Miller. *Political Campaigns.* Mankato, MN: Capstone Press, 2008.

CBS News. "How Many People Attended March For Our Lives? Crowd in DC Estimated at 200,000." March 25, 2018. http://www.cbsnews.com/news/march-for-our-lives-crowd-size-estimated-200000-people-attended-d-c-march.

CBS News. "Iconic Presidential Campaign Moments." Retrieved February 12, 2019. http://www.cbsnews.com/pictures/memorable-presidential-campaign-moments-through-the-years.

Cunningham, Kevin. *How Political Campaigns and Elections Work.* North Mankato, MN: Abdo Publishing, 2015.

De Capua, Sarah. *Running for Public Office.* New York, NY: Children's Press, 2013.

Goodman, Susan E., and Elwood H. Smith. *See How They Run: Campaign Dreams, Election Schemes, and the Race to the White House.* New York, NY: Bloomsbury, 2008.

Gottfried, Jeffrey, and Elisa Shearer. "News Use Across Social Media Platforms 2016." Pew Research Center, May 26, 2016. http://www.journalism.org/2016/05/26/news-use-across-social-media-platforms-2016.

Haest, Cris (founder of Bright Social Agency). Interview with the author in Richardson, Texas, February 11, 2019.

Kirby, Jen. "Read: Attorney General Delivers Summary of Special Counsel's Report." Vox, March 24, 2019. http://www.vox.com/2019/3/24/18279818/mueller-report-attorney-general-summary-conclusions.

Krieg, Gregory. "It's Official: Clinton Swamps Trump in Popular Vote." CNN, December 22, 2016. http://www.cnn.com/2016/12/21/politics/donald-trump-hillary-clinton-popular-vote-final-count/index.html.

League of Women Voters. "How to Judge a Candidate." August 19, 2008. http://www.lwv.org/educating-voters/how-judge-candidate.

Misiroglu, Gina. *The Handy American Government Answer Book.* Canton, MI: Visible Ink Press, 2018.

Morgans, Gareth (political consultant). Interview with the author in Houston, Texas, March 6, 2019.

Pew Research Center. "Election 2016: Campaigns as a Direct Source of News." July 18, 2016. http://www.journalism.org/2016/07/18/election-2016-campaigns-as-a-direct-source-of-news.

Pilkington, Ed. "How Beto O'Rourke Became a Texas Sensation Who Could Shape the Future of the Democrats." *The Guardian*, November 9, 2018. http://www.theguardian.com/us-news/2018/nov/09/beto-o-rourke-ted-cruz-texas-democrats-midterms.

Scardino, Franco. *US Government and Politics.* Indianapolis, IN: Penguin Random House, 2016.

Thomas, William. *How Do We Elect Our Leaders?* Pleasantville, NY: Gareth Stevens Publishing, 2008.

Troy, Gil. "Candidates Take to the Stump, Then and Now." *New York Times*, January 17, 1988. http://www.nytimes.com/1988/01/17/opinion/l-candidates-take-to-the-stump-then-and-now-446188.html.

Wellstone. *Campaign Roles and Responsibilities.* Retrieved February 2, 2019. https://www.wellstone.org/sites/default/files/attachments/Campaign-Roles-and-Responsibilities_0.pdf.

INDEX

A

Adams, John Quincy, 8, 9
advertising, 6, 24, 26, 27
  Facebook, 5
  revenue, 37
Affordable Care Act (ACA), 36, 42
algorithms, 38
analytics, 25

B

bias, political, 34
block walking, 6, 26, 27

C

candidates
  access to, 6, 7, 9, 10–11, 12, 13, 14, 15–16, 18, 20–22, 26–27, 28–29, 30, 32–34, 39, 43–44, 47, 51
  and communications, 6, 16, 20, 23, 24, 25, 26, 27, 29–30, 31, 32, 35, 36, 46
  Donald Trump, 42–43
  Hillary Clinton, 42
  and issues, 48
  and money, 19
  and news, 34, 38, 40–41
  perception of, 14–15, 20, 22
  presidential, 8–9, 11–12, 16, 22, 36
  researching, 48–49
  and social media, 4–5, 6, 17, 27–29, 30, 33, 38, 45, 46
  and voters, 45
city council, 25, 48, 49
Clinton, Hillary, 42
Congress, 23, 25, 48–49
campaigns, 15, 49
consultants, 23
  marketing, 24

D

directors, communications, 24

E

elected officials, 16, 26–27, 30, 33–34, 47, 48, 51
elections, 6, 11–12, 16, 24, 27, 33–34, 39, 45, 48–49
  1828 presidential, 9
  midterm, 18, 48
  2016 presidential, 39, 42, 46
Election Day, 29
electoral college, 42
electorate, 25, 26, 27, 45
experts, 18, 22–23, 24, 25, 46
  communications, 6
  social media, 38

F

Facebook, 6, 33, 44–45
  ads, 5
Facebook Live, 4, 6

fake news, 36–38, 39, 49
field work, 26, 27, 51
Founding Fathers, 13–14
front porch campaigning, 12–13, 31

G

grassroots campaigning, 4
gun control, 48

H

Haest, Chris, 27, 28, 29, 38, 39
Hanna, Mark, 12–13

I

Instagram, 6, 33, 44–45
interviews, 6, 25, 26, 28–29, 30, 39, 41

J

Jackson, Andrew, 8, 9, 10
  and stumping, 43

K

Kennedy, John F., debate with Nixon, 14–15, 20, 43

L

legislation, 36, 42, 47
  gun control, 48
legislative session, 16
legislature, state, 23, 25, 49

M

March for Our Lives movement, 47–48
mayor, 25
McKinley, William, 12–13
media
  attention from, 25, 26
  appearances with, 25
  campaigns, 16
  forms of, 8
  machine, 16–17
  new, 32–33
  physical, 26
  political, 12–13
  relationships with, 24
mudslinging, 8–9

N

newspapers, 6, 7, 8–9, 10, 29, 36
Nixon, Richard, debate with Kennedy, 14–15, 20, 22, 43
nominees, presidential, 9, 10

O

Obama, Barack, 6, 36
  legislation, 42
O'Rourke, Beto, 4–6, 18
  campaign of, 18
  money raised, 18–19
  and social media, 6

P

phone banking, 26, 27
platform, campaign, 29–30, 32–33, 35
policy, 14, 21, 36, 41
political messaging, 4, 35, 36, 51
political party, 9, 10, 18, 27–28
politicians, 9, 13–14, 19, 20–21, 36, 38, 39, 47
popular vote, 42
propaganda, 9, 36, 39
public office, 9, 34, 45, 47, 51

R

radio, 7, 14
railroad travel, 7, 12
rallies, 9, 16, 32–33
Roosevelt, Theodore, 12, 34
  speeches from, 34

S

school board, 25, 48, 49
Snapchat, 33
social media, 4–5, 6, 17, 20–21, 24, 25, 27–29, 30, 31, 33, 37, 38, 39, 42–43, 45, 46, 47, 51
  accounts, 39, 45, 46
  experts, 38, 46
  maelstrom of, 38–39
  management of, 25
  posts, 24
  users of, 38
source, news, 34, 38, 39, 41

specialists, communications, 23, 24, 25, 46
strategy, communications, 5, 6, 9, 12, 13, 16, 20, 23, 24, 27
stumping, 10–14, 43

T

television, 7, 14, 15–16, 21, 29, 42
Trump, Donald, 36, 39, 42
twenty-four-hour news cycle, 31, 34
Twitter, 6, 33, 42, 44–45
  followers, 24

U

unbiased reporting, 9

V

voters, reaching, 6, 10, 12, 13, 14, 16, 17, 18, 20, 21–22, 25, 27–28, 29–30, 31, 32, 41, 42, 45, 51
turnout, 45

W

Webster, Daniel, 10
White, Hugh Lawson 10

Y

yellow journalism, 36–37, 39
YouTube, 20–21, 32–33, 46

ABOUT THE AUTHOR

Angie Timmons is a writer and communications consultant who worked on two US congressional campaigns and one state campaign leading up to the 2018 midterms. She sits on the board of directors and cochairs the communications committee of a women's political group in Texas. She has written multiple books for Rosen, including histories on World War II, the Cold War, the Nanjing Massacre, and racism, with a heavy emphasis on the politics behind those subjects. She lives with her husband and their three cats in the Dallas area.

PHOTO CREDITS

Cover JGI/Jamie Grill/Getty Images; pp. 4–5 (background graphics) weerawan/iStock/Getty Images; pp. 5, 16–17, 22–23 Chip Somodevilla/Getty Images; p. 7 (inset) Bloomberg/Getty Images; p. 8 Bettmann/Getty Images; p. 11 Library of Congress Prints and Photographs; pp. 14–15 CBS Photo Archive/Getty Images; p. 21 Alex Wong/Getty Images; p. 26 Stephanie Keith/Getty Images; p. 28 Joseph Prezioso/AFP/Getty Images; p. 32 Robert Nickelsberg/Archive Photos/Getty Images; p. 33 Joe Skipper/Getty Images; p. 35 Scott Olson/Getty Images; p. 37 Jo Panuwat D/Shutterstock.com; pp. 40–41 EQRoy/Shutterstock.com; p. 43 Mark Ralston/AFP/Getty Images; p. 44 Kerem Yucel/AFP/Getty Images; p. 47 John Lamparski/WireImage/Getty Images; p. 50 Mario Tama/Getty Images; additional graphic elements moodboard - Mike Watson Images/Brand X Pictures/Getty Images (chapter opener backgrounds), Maksim M/Shutterstock.com (fists).

Design: Michael Moy; Editor: Rachel Aimee; Photo Researcher: Nicole DiMella